His Majesty's Service

Love Stories

of a

Caregiver

Dr. G Landry

His Majesty's Service ... Love Stories of a Caregiver
Copyright © 2012 by Dr. G Landry

All rights reserved. No part of this book may be reproduced or transmitted in any form or by any means without written permission of the author.

ISBN-13: 978-0615636139
ISBN-10: 0615636136

Vienna Schilling Books
Fair Oaks, California
www.viennaschilling.us

Printed in the United States of America

Meet the Author

Dr. G Landry is an author, producer, teacher, community activist and, ordained Minister of the Gospel. Born in New Orleans, Louisiana, she is the founder of several ministries and community organizations, among them: WOMEN'S NETWORK FOR CANCER PREVENTION, Helpers for the Homeless and Hungry, Boxes from the Bible Women's Prison Ministry, Reach One Children's Ministry, and Caregivers Speak. She is also the producer of 'Catch the Vision' on Time Warner Cable, Los Angeles. Called of the Lord into the challenging field of care-giving, with supernatural signs following, Dr. Landry shares intimate details of her prolific life and profession, spanning well over three decades. You'll laugh and cry as she takes us along on her journey of love and bravery, beyond the call of duty. There's no other story quite like Dr. Landry's!

Very Special Thanks to the Beloved

Mr. Eli and Mrs. Edythe Broad
Founders of Sun America, Inc.
And their associate, Mr. Warren Smith

Special thanks also to:
Mr. Herb Cobbs
Dr. Doris Morgan
Mr. Willie and Mrs. Lois G. Smith
Mr. Fred and Mrs. Betty Price
Mr. Ed McMahon and Mrs. Pam McMahon
Ms. Carolyn Range and Ms. Diane Palmer
Mrs. Viola Govan
Ms. Sheila Claiborne
Mrs. Sharon Pullard
Rosalind A. Smith

And to all the H.H.H. Helpers:
Mr. E. J. Landry, Jr., Mr. Bruce A. Jackson,
Mrs. Yvonne Marion Harrison,
and Mrs. Thelma King
Without your warm love and generosity,
millions of people would never have been helped!

Thanks also to Selma Kerren for
helping me to coordinate this book.

Table of Contents

Chapter 1	Love's Written Agreement...........	9
Chapter 2	Love in a Cupcake........................	23
Chapter 3	Love in a Spaghetti Pot................	31
Chapter 4	Love in a Suitcase........................	41
Chapter 5	Love in a Wash Bucket................	49
Chapter 6	Love Unconditional......................	59
Chapter 7	No Stranger Love.........................	69
Chapter 8	Love Takes the Call......................	79
Chapter 9	Love's Just Aburnin'.....................	85
Chapter 10	Love Takes Courage.....................	93
Chapter 11	Love is Patient..............................	99
Chapter 12	Love's Endurance.........................	109
Chapter 13	Who Cares for the Caregiver?.....	115

None of us ever asked to be born into abject
poverty, abuse, crime and addiction.
The question is ... what went wrong?
The answer could be, some people never
stood a chance when they were born!

Chapter 1

Love's Written Agreement

Obedience, or submissive compliance, is the act of obeying orders from others. Some might even say: to obey is to be safe. Obedience is also defined this way:

1. The act or practice of following instructions, complying with rules or regulations, or submitting to someone's authority.

2. The religious authority exercised by God, church, a pastor, or another member of the clergy; or those who are under this authority.

Every caregiver should be in compliance with this definition. If not, maybe you should rethink your role as a caregiver.

One day, God woke me up and said, "Go find someone to help," and I replied, "I'm too busy. I have a million and one things to do."

Then that persuasive voice called once again and said, "How can you be too busy when it's my time you are on? Someone needs your help."

I guess that got my attention. Normally, I know and follow the voice of God. To some of us it may be a feeling, or just a knowing, but we follow it, and it's always right.

I had a busy career and was convinced that was what I was supposed to be doing. Not so! When God has your agenda and your destiny planned, it's up to you to be obedient to that voice or feeling and follow the directions. No matter how uncomfortable it may feel or look, you must follow the voice of the Lord.

Shortly thereafter, I came across a scripture that changed everything, and I allowed myself to come into the center of the Lord's will. The Book of Exodus clearly points out the reward.

Love's Written Agreement

> Exodus 23: 22
> "But if you shall indeed obey [my] voice, and do all that I speak, then I will be an enemy to your enemies, and an adversary to your adversaries.

That's when I declared, "God, I want whatever it is that you want for my life today!" Then, I put myself into motion, and never looked back. I always knew from a child that the call of God was on my life to help others. From my earliest years, I remember feeling the emotional pain of my best friends.

When I was growing up, I always wanted to help the other children with their problems, and seemingly had an answer for whatever they were going through. My childhood best friend was Jamie. We were mac' 'n cheese, salt 'n pepper; we were glued to each other.

One of us was hardly ever seen without the other. We were so close, that I always felt her pain. I can remember one day, that we were playing in a vacant lot where both of our mothers told us never to go, but we went there, anyway. Jamie and I were playing and running round, looking for hidden treasures, when we came upon this huge, old tree, and Jamie decided to climb it.

It was as though I saw a movie in front of my face. I saw her falling out of the tree. I warned her not to climb it, but she insisted and continued on ever upward. As she reached the top, she fell, just as I had 'seen' in the flash before my face.

I was obedient to warn her, but she was disobedient in response. Immediately, my head began to hurt and I could not understand it. I was not the one that had fallen.

This was the beginning of many such feelings to come throughout my life. As I grew up, that feeling turned out to be, what is today referred to as, compassion; a compassion for others and their problems and ailments.

I soon learned that obedience must be added to this gift and my daily plans. I was always there for my friends and their families. Into adulthood, this compassion became intrinsic, automatic, and natural as breathing. Before long, obedience to this gift was just as important as the gift itself. Having learned to pair obedience with compassion resulted in the gift of care-giving.

> Isaiah 1:19-20
> "If you be willing and obedient, you shall eat the good of the land: but if you refuse and rebel, you shall be devoured with the sword: for the mouth of the Lord has spoken it."

Obedience really kicked in when my friends needed me, by helping and going above the normal range of assistance. It first began with a special friend. I was away on a business trip one day, and I received a call to come home. My good friend, Naomi, was sick. We were like sisters in our adult life and she was asking for me.

She had become very sick, indeed, with severe pains in her chest and arms. Having been rushed to the hospital, the doctors first thought it was her heart, but after the tests came back, stage-4 breast cancer was discovered. Naturally, she was upset and wanted to know what I thought about the outcome of her medical examination.

Being the close friends that we were, I did not hesitate to come home and went directly to see her in the hospital.

Upon arrival, I saw the sad look on her face, and decided to cheer her up. We laughed about the good times we use to have, then we cried about what was happening to her, and then we prayed to God, coming into agreement for her healing. We talked well into the night and I stayed with her throughout the ordeal.

Although her doctor insisted on immediate action and told her it was crucial that they operate right away, she did not commit to surgery until several weeks later. After the surgery, the doctor pronounced the devastating news that nothing more could be done for my friend, Naomi. He said, "I got as much of it as I could."

Back in those days, medical science wasn't as sophisticated as it is today. They did not have the medical technology they have today. Frequently, doctors butchered women's bodies so badly, that many were left severely disfigured. Such was the case with Naomi. After surgery, my sweet friend was so very disfigured that her husband could not stand to look at her any more. This made her very depressed and shattered her self esteem. In addition, the American Cancer Society, one of the few places of support, failed to recognize women of color back then.

We, the friends of Naomi were her true support. Having fallen into a very deep depression, it seemed like nothing we did would ever bring her out of it. At this juncture, the true meaning of care-giving set in. I was about to become a true caregiver.

During chemo-therapy, Naomi was always in pain, and she vomited all the time. I held her and prayed over her. I took her to the medical appointments, to chemo-treatments, and I watched her become sicker and sicker. By then, her husband walked out on her, unable to cope with the pressure of his wife being so very sick; nor could he stand to look at her disfigured body. We all have the ability to be a caregiver, but some choose not to.

I always thought marriage was supposed to be, "Through sickness and health, until death do us part," and yet I watched this marriage crumble before my eyes.

His Majesty's Service

I really could not understand it. Only then did I realize that everyone does not have the capacity to be a caregiver. After her husband left, Naomi became homeless, so I moved her in with me. I could not let her die on the streets of Los Angeles and continued to take care of her; praying most of the time and reading the word of God to her, but I could see she was slipping away. There was nothing else I could do.

I began a regiment of raw-juicing for her. I made cold drinks and hot soups and juiced every green thing that I could find; spinach, greens, kale, everything green! Most days she did not want to eat, but I made her take in as much as possible every day. Although I saw that she was beginning to improve, if only for the moment, I watched her become thinner and thinner, until the day she could no longer swallow. I knew then that her time was near.

But, I continued to take care of her, anyway. I was her caregiver. I changed her dressings, and her diapers. It was very hard for me to see someone I cared about waste away to nothing, but God gave me the sustaining power to carry on. I simply would not turn my back on her.

Love's Written Agreement

Naomi was my very best friend. We grew up together, went to school together, laughed and cried together. We were always there for each other. So it was automatically natural for me to be her caregiver.

This gives a different meaning to the word caregiver. Long before the term 'caregiver' became popular as it is today, we were simply providing care for those we loved. I did not think of being called a caregiver back then. I just shared my love with a friend. I shared all that I could to make her happy.

When her doctors ordered her back into the hospital, I thought that was it; but she fought and fought, and then they sent her home again. This time, the doctors said that the cancer had taken over her entire body, and there was nothing more they could do. They wanted to put her into a home to die. Instead, I brought her back home with me. I continued to take care of her at home, with me, in happy loving surroundings. This went on for the next five months. On November 4, 1970, Naomi went home to be with the Lord.

I felt as though I had lost a sister. And now I, the strong and steadfast care-giver, was lost and at a crossroad. I could not believe she was gone. I could not understand that, even though we prayed and agreed for her healing, she still died. But I failed to realize that it was her will, her time and her destiny. First, the cancer was in her body too long prior to detection, second she had no symptoms of the cancer, or maybe she just ignored them. Naomi was the second woman in my lifetime to die from cancer.

The situation gave me new respect for obedience. I looked at this event and saw that, had I not been obedient to what God wanted me to do, my friend would have died alone, perhaps on the streets. We must always keep in the front of our minds the Lord's admonishment. Obedience is better than sacrifice. Sometimes caregivers forget to obey and they loose sight of what they are supposed to do. When we listen to that small voice, we know there will be a price to pay.

Love's Written Agreement

> 1st Samuel 15:22
> And Samuel said, "Has the Lord as great delight in burned offerings and sacrifices, as in obeying the voice of the lord? Behold, to obey is better than sacrifice, and to harken is better than the fat of rams.

Sometimes caregivers forget to obey and they lose sight of what they are supposed to do; but if we listen to that still, small voice we know there will be a sacrifice to pay if we don't obey. How many times have you driven along and that small voice said to you, "Turn here," but you turned the other way instead, and encountered a bad situation. Had you obeyed that small voice, you could have avoided that accident, or getting lost, or the flat tire, and so forth.

This is why I believe strongly, "Obedience is better than sacrifice." It's always better to obey and stay in front of any unforeseen danger.

As caregivers, you may not always want to clean the poop off a love one, nor change their diaper, but God will give you the grace you need to hold onto the obeying spirit He placed inside of you. Learn to trust God and trust what's ahead of you, in all your caring for others.

Love in a Cupcake

Chapter 2

Love in a Cupcake

Grace is defined in the English North America Encarta Dictionary in several ways, but the one which most closely describes a caregiver's personality is 'generosity of spirit' followed by:

> A capacity to tolerate, accommodate, and forgive people.

I was much younger when my grandmother passed away from cancer; however, I remember how much compassion she had for others. My grandmother was a slender, well dressed, soft-spoken woman. In fact, she was the epitome of grace. She was kind, and always had a friendly disposition from which her kindly acts flowed.

His Majesty's Service

As an insurance agent, she used to take me with her to collect her clients' insurance money. Along these errands, whenever she encountered anyone in need, she went to the store to buy groceries and would leave them at the family's door, without ever letting them know it was her that left them. My grandmother was full of grace and truth.

I didn't understand it then, but I truly do get it today. She did it as unto the Lord, not to be seen of men. I admired my grandmother with everything in my being. She was a good woman; a very intelligent and smart woman.

She knew how to conduct business well and I always learned something new from her. I enjoyed it when she took the time to explain how her insurance business worked, and why she cared for her clients.

I enjoyed staying at Grandma's house because while there, I always got delicious treats. I remember she made these little 'hoe cakes' for me. We would stay up late at night in the kitchen as I watched her make these delights for me.

I learned many things from her, which I took with me into adulthood, among them: grace, kindness and giving. It was her kindly acts from which proceeded loving-kindness and general goodwill.

Then, I watched her suffer in bed at home from cancer. I can still remember being in the room with her, hearing her moan and groan. I would rub her head and say to her, "It's going to be okay, mama."

I can also remember telling her that I was going to do something about care-giving one day. Since then, I immersed myself into helping, not only women with cancer, but homeless women, street people, hungry children, orphans, the elderly and widows.

"Pure religion and undefiled before the Father," said the Apostle James in 1:27, "Is to visit the fatherless and widows in their affliction, and to keep one's self unspotted from the world."

My grandmother was the first person I actually watched die of cancer. From that experience, God placed in me an uncontrollable compassion for others. I didn't know at the time what care-giving was, but that particular situation provided me with insight on how to proceed later in life.

It was also God's grace that upheld us through her sickness.

A very long time ago, loved ones were kept at home with their families and were allowed to die at home. They were not put away somewhere cold and impersonal. I watched my mother and her sister (my Aunt Bobbie) take care of my grandmother when she was dying, with the daily acts of true love and care-giving.

> Hebrews 4:16
> Let us therefore come boldly to the throne of grace, so that we may obtain mercy and find grace to help in time of need.
>
> 2nd Corinthians 12:9
> And He said to me, "My grace is sufficient for you: for my strength is made perfect in weakness."

Love in a Cupcake

Therefore, no matter how weak you may feel being a caregiver, know that it's not you caring for someone. It is always the Lord working through you, and his grace is always sufficient for you to carry on.

Love in a Spaghetti Pot

Chapter 3

Love in a Spaghetti Pot

In 1970, God gave me the vision of a women's network for cancer prevention. He said, "Speak to women and help them to prevent cancer in their bodies."

One night during my prayer time, I felt the Lord's physical presence next to me. That's when He spoke to me again and gave me more complete instructions. It was as if He was right next to me in the room. Shortly thereafter, He showed me the logo on the wall of my bedroom. It freaked me out completely! I saw the logo of the organization I was to start up right there on my wall. The acronyms were W.N.C.P, which stood for WOMEN'S NETWORK FOR CANCER PREVENTION.

The logo design was to be a square with a small cross inside. I saw it in color and it was a beautiful green against the white wall. I explained what I saw to a very gifted, young lady, and she gave form to the vision by designing the beautiful logo of W.N.C.P.

As the vision came into fruition, God was saying to me, "You are my caregiver, and I will provide for you." I continued to pray and fast, to be sure that it was God leading.

During this time, I worked for the City of Los Angeles, and seeing nothing in place for women of color, I knew that I had to do something about it. So I began to conduct informational meetings on weekends to inform women of low income and of color about organizational resources, which addressed the cancer quandary.

This was my first embrace of the cancer community. These meetings were followed-up with breast self-exam classes, and I put together an informative booklet for women of color to explain how to do their own breast self-examination.

The booklet is called **Black Americans and Cancer** and you can request a free copy, by mailing your request to the address included at the end of this book. You pay for postage only.

My associates and I still use both publications today to educate young women on the importance of breast self-examination. While working for the city, and watching the homeless numbers escalate, people in authority appeared to be at a loss for what to do. Most of the L.A. officials saw the situation as a cash-cow, as mountains of federal dollars poured in for poverty programs, and as usual, went nowhere.

Void of a real solution for helping, I naturally felt the pain of the thousands of people looking for help. Although food was necessary for their survival, they needed more than that. Therefore, in 1974, the Lord gave me yet another ministry name and concept: Helpers for the Homeless and Hungry (HHH).

The vision expanded and eventually occupied an entire city block on West Slauson Avenue, in Los Angeles.

His Majesty's Service

The HHH Community Center offered many valuable services, consisting of a daily hot-meal program and weekly grocery distribution, which were the highlight of our donor activities.

The Center also hosted a thrift store where the needy received clothing free of charge, and was also open for the community to come in and purchase name-brand clothing at very low prices. To help disenfranchised persons integrate back into the work force, the center also offered a computer center with job training and, best of all, individual shower stalls where they could come in and get cleaned up.

Highlighted programs each year were the 'Annual Thanksgiving Feeding in the Park' coordinated by the employees of Sun America, Inc. And for children, the late, great Ed McMahon, and his lovely wife Pam, headed up our 'Annual Toy Giveaway' at Christmas.

HHH also offered counseling in anger management, domestic violence, job preparation and drug counseling; plus a recycling center where the community came in to sell their glass and aluminum products. It was quite the hub of divine activity in its day. These operations involved a lot of large-scale funding and we were glad to receive it.

Taking care of the hungry and homeless was a life-changing experience, through which the concept of care-giving took on a whole new prospective. It was during this experience that taking care of someone you know, and who is related to you, is one thing; but it's a whole different story if it's someone you don't know.

I was helping total strangers, people I had never seen before; people who had all types of problems. It seemed as if God hand-picked these situations just for me to hover over. You have to be a true care-giver to work with these types of people. In fact, you have to give your all. Just when you felt like there was no more to give, you had to rest, pray up, and go back in strong.

In the early days when I helped the street people, there were no rules of what and how to do it. One night in 1974, I ventured out into the streets of downtown Los

Angeles with a large pot of spaghetti, and the word in my mouth.

Proverbs 19: 17 rang out in my head, and I could not let it go. Later, this became the scripture I held fast to, for my work with the poor.

> Proverbs 19:17
> He that has pity upon the poor lends to the Lord, and that which he has given will the Lord pay him back."

That night down at skid-row, I parked my car and attempted to step out with my big pot of spaghetti, and just then, God sent an angel to assist me. A security guard from a nearby mission came over and said that he saw me drive up in my Mercedes, and thought I was either crazy, or there to buy drugs. A Mercedes on skid-row just didn't look right to him. As we began talking, he soon found out that neither was true. He understood that I was on a mission from God.

Skid-row's street people saw that I had hot food, and naturally, they wanted to eat. The guard got the crowd into an orderly line and assisted me as I served hot food from my trunk of my car.

The Lord directed me to count the paper plates before I got started, and that first night, I served over one hundred people. I had no idea that one large pot of spaghetti would ever go so far ... but He knew!

After I finished the 'spaghetti service' the guard waited until I was safely in my car, and I told the crowd that I would be back soon. When I got home, I called a friend and explained what had happened. It was a true divine appointment from God in every sense. The Lord had revealed to me another side of care-giving. Then I began to pray and ask God what this divine evening was all about? What did He want from me? I could not understand what it was that I was supposed to do.

Then, I began to feel the various pains of the people on the streets. My legs and feet began to hurt as though I walked all day long. I begin to have bad headaches, and I was never one to get headaches before that. Then, I suffered chills in the heat of summer, for which there was no explanation because I wasn't sick. That's when I realized the Lord was giving me an inclination of the various pains of those I prayed for out on the street. I began to see their faces and continued to pray for them on a daily basis.

God had a plan, and it unfolded immediately. Within two weeks after I first went downtown to feed the hungry from a spaghetti pot in the back of my car, God gave me a kitchen! Then, everything seemed to come in overnight. Food poured in from everywhere, and everything I needed to operate a kitchen just suddenly appeared.

I had a place to prepare the food and was able to serve more than two hundred and fifty people at a time!

I began to hold meetings in Black communities to inform residents as to the plight of their brothers and sisters. God assembled a workforce to assist me with the downtown skid-row project.

Love in a Suitcase

Chapter 4

Love in a Suit Case

Mercy is a compassionate action or treatment, or relief from distress. Mercy is part of God's character, and He wants this to be part of our character also. Mercy is cause for hope.

In 1865, Abraham Lincoln declared in his Washington, D.C., speech that he was preparing the United States for life after the U.S. Civil War. During that speech, he said something very humble and succinct.

"I have always found that mercy bears richer fruits than strict justice."

> Micah 6: 8
> He has shown you, oh man, what is good: and what does the Lord require of you, but to do justly, and to love mercy, and to walk humbly with your God.

It was mercy, therefore, that arose within me with the mandate from God, to feed, cloth and educate people who had nothing. For this reason, I held more monthly meetings to bridge the gap between the homeless community and medical entities.

As a result, more homeless women became educated on breast cancer, received assistance for medical conditions, and learned where they can go for help. Although the public at large still cannot envision the two together, there is nevertheless a strong connection between health issues and homelessness.

By then, I was giving lectures not just to small communities but to thousands, and I felt the true impact of Matthew Chapter 25. In fact, God took me around the world to help others.

Love in a Suitcase

Matthew 25: 35-40

For I was hungry, and you gave Me something to eat. I was thirsty, and you gave Me something to drink. I was a stranger and you took Me in; naked, and you clothed Me; sick and you visited Me. I was in prison, and you visited Me.

Then shall the righteous answer him, saying, "Lord, when did we see you hungry, and feed you? When were you thirsty and we gave you to drink, or saw you as a stranger, and took you in? When did we see you naked, and clothe you? Or, sick and in prison and we visited you?

Then, the King shall answer, "Assuredly I say to you, inasmuch as you have done it to the least of these, my brethren, you have done it to Me."

His Majesty's Service

One day, I received a letter from London, England. The letter came from a group of London-based organizations, requesting me to come and lecture on the programs I had set up in California.

The writing party wanted to learn how they too could bridge the gap between women's health issues and homelessness. So, my colleagues and I traveled to the U.K. and held a three-day conference wherein the British people from all over the U.K obtained information on how ways to set up their own mission programs for destitute women living on the street.

From there, we travelled to Jamaica, Haiti, St. Croix, Kenya, Namibia and Johannesburg in Africa. When we arrived in Africa, it seemed as if God shifted into high gear, because we weren't just dealing with cancer and homelessness. We were faced with the much larger issue of Human Immunodeficiency Virus (HIV) and Acquired Immune Deficiency Syndrome (AIDS).

This is when we started caring for children. We encountered an overwhelming number of children infected with AIDS that were homeless because their parents, who were also infected, had already died. It seems as though God sent everyone in the world to me for one reason or another. I felt myself caring for people I knew nothing about; people who spoke different languages, and yet, somehow we managed to communicate. Whenever I entered into a new country, very good interpreters were always with me.

Somehow the people knew I was there to offer help. Some were celebrities, others were orphans, abused women, widows, homeless people living on the streets, women with cancer, and many others. They all needed something that I had to give. It was while caring for these people that the love of God made all things possible.

Love in a Wash Bucket

Chapter 5

Love in a Wash Bucket

I recall another event wherein I started out caring for one woman which blossomed into touching thousands of men, women and children, in a world where those people were totally forgotten!

On this particular day, God himself gave me yet another mandate. He told me to go and wash the feet of the people living on the streets!

Wow! That went over great. Everyone that I told about this thought I was crazy. They said, "You're out of your mind! You've really lost it this time!"

In fact, I got such a negative response, that even I began to doubt God, but when you are stepping out in faith and 'practicing' obedience, doubting God can be very detrimental. We must never doubt him.

My doubting, reminded me of the time when Peter walked on the water toward the Lord on the tempest lake; but then he took his eyes off the Lord and started to sink.

> Matthew 14: 31
> And immediately Jesus stretched forth his hand, caught Peter, and said to him, "Oh you, of little faith; why did you doubt?"

During this time, I found myself looking for reasons not to do this, so I called a pastor of my longtime acquaintance and told him what God had said, but he told me what I actually did not want to hear.

"If God said it, then do it."

When God gives a mandate, it must be fulfilled, no mater how crazy it seems to others. Notice that He told me to wash the feet of those on skid-row, not my other associates and there was a reason for that. Because of their unbelief, now we know why.

Knowing that God has told you to do something, you had better obey and do it. Obedience is much better than sacrifice. And then God supplied me with all the tools necessary to take on this task.

Immediately after that, an avalanche of donated supplies thundered in: disinfectors, gloves; clean, new socks, the pails to wash their feet in, and even the water! Everything I needed for the job had been put before me. Now all I needed to do was accept the task and do it.

So I told my staff again what God showed me to do with a new conviction, and they of course, looked at me again as though I had lost my mind. Then, we prayed and set out for Los Angeles' skid-row to feed and wash the feet of the homeless. It was a memorable Saturday afternoon that we'll never forget.

Upon arrival, we proceeded as usual to set up for the feeding. On the sidewalk, I set up a chair along with all the items God gave me to wash the people's feet.

I got down on my knees and began to pray. As I poured the water into the pail, the people began to come.

One man asked, "What are you going to do with that water?" I looked up at him and said, "I'm going to wash the people's feet."

He looked at me with disbelief, so I asked if he would like his feet washed. And he replied with a big smile on his face, "Yes."

He was an older, white man with very dirty clothes, and no shoes. His feet were in very bad shape, and encrusted with black crud and sores. The water was warm and filled with disinfectors. As he sat down he continued to ask me, "Why are you doing this?" I looked up at him and said, "God told me to do so."

As I washed his feet, I began to pray in the spirit, thanking God for this man's healing and deliverance. So I washed and prayed, and washed and prayed. I had to change the water four times before the natural color of the white man's feet became visible.

Love in a Wash Bucket

After I washed his feet and saw the true color of his skin, it seemed as though there was a silk coating on his feet. His sores had closed up! Momentarily, it scared me, but then I realized God had just healed his feet!

That day, the old white man with black, encrusted feet accepted Christ as his personal Lord and Savior. Because his feet were so dirty, he must have thought I would never touch them. He started out in disbelief but four wash buckets later, the man walked away as a Believer!

After him, the people lined up one by one up, received the Lord into their hearts, and before I knew it, I was washing the feet of God's children. Everyone who sat in that chair was prayed over and received the Lord as their savior. It was a miracle on skid-row that day.

If someone had told me a year earlier to go downtown and start washing feet on skid- row, on my hands and knees no less, I would have told them to go jump in the lake. But I knew that it was all God, so I had no reservations doing it. People came from near and far to see the lady on her knees washing people's dirty feet.

Another incredible thing happened that day. One homeless woman sat in the chair smoking drugs! With a crack pipe in her right hand and a lighter in the left, she was loud and very obnoxious. In fact, she acted like the Queen of Egypt wanting me to peel her grape!

However, once she put both feet into the water, it was all over for her. I began to pray in the spirit, and suddenly, by an unseen force, the pipe flew out of her hand in one direction, and the lighter in another. God delivered her of drug addiction on the spot and she began to cry uncontrollably. She too received the Lord as personal Savior.

Another man sat in the chair and at first he would not say anything at all. As I washed his feet, he began to cry. I looked up and saw tears streaming down his cheeks. I asked him what was wrong and he explained that he had killed a man, and could not sleep because of this traumatic event. He could not sleep and walked around all day and night paralyzed in the headlock grip of guilt and torment.

Love in a Wash Bucket

So, I prayed with this tormented soul and told him that he had to confess and turn himself into the police.

I told him that once he does this, he will have peace, and he agreed to do so. As I dried his feet and put a clean pair of white socks on him, he got up and started walking toward the local police station not far from our chair and bucket.

> Malachi 3: 7
> "Even from the days of your fathers you are gone away from my ordinances, and have not kept them. Return to me, and I will return to you," says the Lord of Hosts. "But you said, 'Wherein shall we return?'"

Washing the people's feet down at skid-row was unconditional love; bad feet, bad smells, no questions asked. Every person that sat in the chair that day was drawn by the Holy Spirit. Everyone had a story to tell, and received Christ or rededicated their life to him. They left with clean feet, a clean pair of white socks, a renewed spirit and clean heart.

Just about everyone who sat in the chair that day was transformed into a new creation by the time they stood up. People came from near and far to get their feet washed, or so they thought. By the end of the day, I was so very weak, I had to be helped up off the ground and placed into the car. In fact, I was weak for a couple of days after that, and could do nothing but sleep and pray.

It was an experience that I and my staff will never forget. God moved in powerful ways. It wasn't me washing their feet; it was the Lord intervening in their lives.

Love Unconditional

Chapter 6

Love Unconditional

The meaning of the word 'unconditional' is: without conditions or reservations; absolute acceptance.

Being a caregiver requires much unconditional love. You have to love whom you are helping, despite of themselves, without conditions. Sometimes, the ones we are assigned to help are rude and out of control and cause us to entertain second thoughts; but we must continue to show God's love...unconditionally.

Often, unconditional love is associated with misbehaved children, family members and friends, drug-users, and others behaving badly. We women also associate unconditional love with our misbehaving husbands.

It was unconditional love directing my steps to help the people of skid-row. They looked bad and smelled bad and many of them acted out while we were trying to help them. It was the love of God in us that reached out to feed, clothe, wash, talk to and even hug them.

In caring for others, caregivers use unconditional love in cases when the recipients are out of control. Let's examine a few problems that caregivers encounter.

In one case, a lady verbally abused me so badly that it cut deep into to my core. It took all I had to hold back tears, because I knew that she was the one that needed help.

She was shoeless, tattered and barely covered. I saw that we did not have any more shoes to give out, so I took off my own shoes and put them on her feet. And God made them to fit perfectly, as if they were made for her! (They were one of my favorites.) God will test you to see if you can deal with unconditional situations. That's the test of a good caregiver.

Love Unconditional

We did have clean clothing to put on her, however, so we redressed her. She began to calm down and eventually cried. God penetrated her heart.

I also remember a homeless mother with girls. I took her into one of my homes with her children, unconditionally. All they needed was a place stay with a roof over their heads; that was all ... just safety from the streets. No shelter could take them in because there were not enough beds available for all of them. Personally, I would have put them on the floor, rather than turn them out!

The shelter would have separated them, anyway, and I felt that was wrong, so I took her and the children into my house. It turned out to be a complete success story. She was able to go back to work and her children were happy living in a safe, stable home environment. Kids need so little to thrive.

Today, I am proud to say that this young woman has GRADUATED FROM COLLEGE with a Bachelor of Arts Degree and is now teaching classes at her church. Her children have also graduated from high school and are also in college. I had to set rules and show unconditional love in order for her to succeed. Unconditional love only helps in situations when we allow God to show up. God shows us this when we are chosen by him, and we all know when those times are.

> Psalms 25:18
> Look upon my affliction and pain; and forgive all my sins.

I heard many stories that day. It was as if these people were waiting for God to show up to hear their confessions. They did not care who was watching or listening to what they were saying. It was more than a foot wash for them. They were being bathed, perhaps for the first time in their lives, in the Lord's unconditional love.

Unconditional love changes the diapers of a fully grown adult, bathes and feeds them. It has unconditional patience for the Alzheimer's patient during times when they lapse into yet another episode of memory loss and schizophrenia. Unconditional love also embraces misbehaving children. Many times we want to go back to old school and take a belt to their bottoms, but in such times we must show them unconditional love.

With much prayer and supplication everything changes, including children. Children learn by example. So when we explain to them what unconditional love is and what it represents, it allows them to know why they cannot have that new iPod, new cell phone, or new, designer clothing. Although it hurts, the experience is good for them.

Unconditional love also applies to irritating family members, like those who use you, or consume drugs. At times you will feel that you cannot take another minute of it. They are sleeping on your couch, stealing money out of your wallet, hardly ever try to find work, eat all your food, and you just can't take it anymore. That's when you have to take another step, and another one after that, to show them unconditional love.

Help where and when you can, and know when to draw the line. I know that right about now some of you are saying, "Well, I'm tired of helping them because they're still doing the same thing over and over. I'm tired of them stealing from me and the family."

Don't give up, keep praying and holding on to God's word for their life. Hold on and don't let go. This is the best situation to display God's unconditional love to them.

Take for instance pastors. Everyone knows that pastors must show unconditional love to those that are hard to handle in their own church, and people that are disagreeable, and many times downright unruly. Pastors have to deal with Christians that believe only they should lead the song that Sunday morning, and those who think they should conduct Bible study today just to be seen by all. Pastors must also extend unconditional love to those who demand to sit on the front row in 'their assigned seat' (they come in extra early just to claim it), and those who come in fashionably late, because they like to be seen by all as they saunter in. Yeah, you know who you are.

Unconditional love makes the world go round. It's a basic need for survival, and must be incorporated into our daily life. It's also nothing new. In an article from Biblical Discernment Ministries, December, 1997, the concept was well presented by the writer.

> "Perhaps one could say that God's love for the Christian is unconditional since the Christian partakes of his love and grace through faith. Wouldn't it be better to say that the conditions have been met? Jesus met the first condition, to wash away the sin that God hates. The believer meets the second condition, but only by God's grace through faith. Perhaps it would be better to say that God's love extended to a person, is conditional by his plan to give eternal life to those whom he has enabled to believe on his son. The conditions of God's love are resident within himself."

The caregiver's love is unconditional. Love is sometimes blind, and that's what makes it unconditional.

Unconditional love is when a daughter goes beyond the call of duty to take care of her mother or father, giving all of her self unconditionally. Unconditional, is a wife sitting up night after night watching her husband suffer from pain.

Total love is without motive or reward.

It can be very hard on our mental state of mind, however, and we can perhaps reach back into our roots and remember other caregivers in our own family. I remember how grandma' kept grandpa' from going into the rest-home for the elderly and infirm. I remember how she cared for him no matter how tired she was after coming home from work. We often heard her sing doing her chores on those tired nights

Although grandma' cared for everyone else, she always seemed to act as though some unseen person cared for her. I knew from a young age that it was the Lord. Yet there are some of you out there who just don't understand the true meaning of the word unconditional.

So let's stop complaining about what you don't have and what you would like to have and begin to seek where you can share your unconditional love with another.

No Stranger Love

Chapter 7

No Stranger Love

Yes, the love of God has always sustained caregivers, as they go in and out of situations. A caregiver cannot operate without love in their heart. Neither can they operate without God's love comforting them.

> Jeremiah 31: 3
> Yea, I have loved you with an everlasting love; therefore with loving kindness have I drawn you."

Some people have a very hard time understanding how a caregiver can show so much love for the demanding people they help. The fact is, it's really simple. Deuteronomy illuminates it this way:

> Deuteronomy 10: 19
> Love therefore the strangers: for you were
> once the strangers in the land of Egypt."

In scriptural terms, Egypt is a symbol of our lives without God, during that time when we were the ones that needed help. Loving strangers may sometimes seem difficult but it's really not that hard. Let's say you meet a good-looking stranger, one that might be a good soul mate for you in marriage, and a certain attraction begins. Often, he or she is the stranger that you fall in love with. Well, that is similar to the caregiver experiencing a love for the recipient, only it's the Lord being in love with them, through the caregiver. Then you must ask yourself this succinct question:

Where is your Egypt? Is it in your home, job, community, or church?

In other words, you were once a stranger when the Lord God began to love you. We cannot be caregivers without loving, nor can we be without love in our hearts.

No Stranger Love

John 13: 34
A new commandment I give to you, that you love one another; as I have loved you, so should you also love one another.

To be a caregiver, love has to be your first motive. It takes a special person to be a caregiver. You are that special person. Don't doubt yourself. You have more love to give than you can imagine. You just have to release it in a positive way. Some of you will have to begin to first love yourselves. When you love yourself, then it's really easy to pass that love on. I have a daily exercise. I look in the mirror and say to the person looking back at me. "Girl, I love you! You are really special."

Remember, you can't project what you don't have. Love heals all wounds. You can also tell the Lord on a daily basis, "Thank you for allowing me to love others as you do." Your heart and mind will hear your spoken declaration and increase your love for humanity.

I love all people, especially strangers. I get a great satisfaction from taking a shattered life and making it whole. It makes me feel as though God appears before the very eyes of all I touch.

I remember one stranger, a young lady, that came into our center as we were praying one morning, and the love of God surrounded her as soon as she stepped through the door. She began to weep and accepted Christ; then she was filled with the Holy Spirit on the spot. It was truly the love of God manifest. I don't take the credit for anything that happens. Today the young lady has a relationship with God, studies and teaches his word daily.

I have seen the practically impenetrable attitude of gang members change right before my eyes, simply because I showed them the love of God. One afternoon, I was in Van Ness Park, where there was a large gathering of gang members. As I walked through them, I felt the love of God overtake me, and I just *had to* say something. So I walked right into the *very middle* of them.

I turned and told one of the young men to pull his pants up. I thought I was going to be jumped at that moment. Some of them cussed me out, while others told them to shut up. The young man whom I told to pull up his pants hung his head down and did not reply, so I went over to him and hugged him. I told him that I wasn't trying to disrespect him in front of his homies, but I loved him and God did as well. He looked at me with tears in his eyes and I knew God had really touched him. That day, I had no idea that he was actually the leader of the gang...but God knew.

I told him who I was, and he remembered that I was the lady from HHH (Helpers for the Homeless and Hungry); the lady that helped people in his community. He told me that he 'had my back' and then he told his homies that nothing was to happen to me. I told him, "Thank you, but I also know that God has my back and nothing is going to happen to me, because God has me on assignment." It seemed he understood that kind of covenant. He shared the same covenant with his homies.

Because I showed love to these young strangers, the presence of God immediately manifested and stood in the midst of us that day in the park. I gave everyone who wanted one, a hug, and told them that I loved them.

His Majesty's Service

The power of love will defuse anything, even the cold shoulder of a stranger. From that day forward, I had the respect of some of the most sought-after gang members in Los Angeles, and all because I stepped into a stranger-situation. The love of God is so very powerful.

It goes where angels fear to tread.

On another occasion, I remember two young strangers, men who did not have a place to stay, and I took them in. Everyone told me I was crazy, because I did not know their backgrounds, nor did I know what they were capable of. However, I never see the reality of a situation or a person; I see only the end result.

I once again trusted in my 'God feeling' and decided to help them. They stayed for over six months during this time I poured the love of God all over them. They just needed to know that someone loved them, that they mattered to somebody somewhere, and that they had a chance in life. Instead of condemning them, I taught them principles of integrity and how to be honest, young men.

No Stranger Love

I made them go to church. Anyone staying in my house eating, sleeping, showering, watching television, so on and so forth, must go to church and school for that matter. They must become responsible members of the household and pick up their share of household chores on a daily basis.

One of the main reasons why so many of our children join gangs is because they are looking for the love they never received early in life. Love your children and other children well.

The result was, the older of these two young men, was blessed with a good job and then he actually met a nice, young lady at church. They were later married. The younger of the two, went on to college, received a basketball scholarship, and is doing very well, indeed. Where would these two young men be had I not taken them in? Still out of the streets of wasted humanity with no chance in life whatsoever!

You just never know how love will affect the perfect stranger. You just have to step out and love them with no stranger love.

I discovered early that it doesn't cost a thing to share and show love. It's real and it's powerful. Love conquers all.

Love

    L - is for the long-lasting love

    O - is for the overwhelming love

    V - is for the victory of love

    E - is for the energy love brings

Put it all together and it spells 'love.' Love everyone you come in contact with. Remember you don't have to like everyone you meet, but you must love them.

Love your enemies and pray for them daily. It's better to love than to hate. Love conquers all.

Love Takes the Call

Chapter 8

Love Takes the Call

Caregivers must be willing to go for it; go for the end of the rainbow. Take a look on the other side of the windshield and see the power of God pouring out in front of you. Willingness is a part of your destiny in life. You must be willing to take chances, go beyond your boundaries and come out of your comfort zone. Caregiving requires free will at all times. Willingness is a sign of obedience, and should be practiced at all times.

I remember the willingness of my heart. I had just came back from vacation and hadn't even unpacked my bags when I got a phone call, that another very dear friend of mine, one whom I considered a brother, was rushed to the hospital. Without hesitation I went to him and his wife. It was the willingness of God in me that gave me the strength to drive eighty miles to the hospital, and the willingness of my heart to stay all night, sitting up in a chair praying over them, while being jet lagged.

> 1st chronicles 28: 9-10
> And you, Solomon My son, must know the God of your father; serve him with a perfect heart and with a willing mind. For the Lord searches all hearts, and understands all the imaginations of the thoughts. If you seek Him, He will be found of you; but if you forsake Him, He will cast you off forever. Take heed now, for the Lord has chosen you to build a house for his sanctuary. Be strong and do it.

A willing heart makes room for your gifts. In the parking lot, before I entered the hospital, I saw a woman crying. I went over to her and consoled her. She was so upset that I don't believe she heard a single word I said; but I persisted and kept on talking until she finally acknowledged me and said, "Thank you."

Love Takes the Call

I prayed with her and assured her that God was the healer. I told her that no matter what the doctors said, it's really all about what God says at the end. She stopped crying, hugged me and squeezed me very tightly and said, "I know God sent you to this parking lot just for me."

You see, my willingness kicked in at that moment. Even though I was there for my brother and his wife, God used me because of my willingness to help someone else.

> 1st timothy 6: 17-18
> God, gives us richly all things to enjoy; so that [we will] do good and be rich in good works; ready to distribute, willing to communicate.

Caregivers must incorporate willingness into their daily lives in order for God's opportunities to present themselves. I saw the willingness of my friend's wife to give up her daily preoccupations and go out and do his job for him, while he was unable to do so.

His Majesty's Service

God will always give us exceeding and abundant strength to do everything, over and above anything we can imagine.

As caregivers, we must be willing to go over and above the call of duty. You may not want to clean a sick person's soiled clothing, beddings or wash their bodies, but the willing heart makes it all go a little smoother. Your obedience to God allows the spirit of willingness to spring forth as the morning dew.

Your spirit might be willing, but your body may not be. Yes fatigue can overtake you, but look for the inward strength and draw from that.

Love's Just Aburnin'

Chapter 9

Love's Just Aburnin'

Many caregivers feel burned out at one point of time or another in their lives. When we get tired of an assignment, the first thing we tend to confess is that we have developed a bad case of 'burnout.'

You know that you are getting 'burnout' when things start to irritate you more readily. When you lose interest in the well-being of the person(s) you are caring for; that's when you know you've got burnout.

I have spoken to many caregivers and they all agreed that long-time care can cause one to burnout. It's the daily routine of the care, the dressing, feeding, cleaning, cooking, and bathing over and over.

They all agree that the sheer repetition and hard labor of it all was many times too overwhelming for just one person to undertake. But I don't see it that way.

I see burnout as a

BURN-IN.

Yes, that's right!

Love is just ABURNIN' to do the will of God!

- Burnin' to shed his love abroad everywhere!

- Burnin' with his word to share it instantly!

- Burnin' with visions of miracles to come!

- Burnin' to strive ever-onward!

- Burnin' to display his power in all the earth.

- Burnin' with longing for his presence

Love's Just Aburnin'

God's power is greater than nuclear power. And with free access to that kind of power, there are no limits to what you can accomplish!

> Exodus 15: 2
> The Lord is my strength and song, and He has become my salvation. He is my God, and I will prepare for Him an habitation; my Father God, I will exalt Him.

How beautiful are those words. They were written by someone whose heart burned with love for God. When you come into the presence of the Lord on days you are burned out, listen closely. He will not tell you to go on, until you are sufficiently recharged!

Recharging is so very important. Without it you can't go on. Recharging allows you to rethink and recover, and put things into proper perspective. If you fail to recharge regularly, you may lose sight of your reasons for care-giving. Recharging helps to refill your inner supply of love and patience.

His Majesty's Service

Don't be fooled into thinking that you never have to get away and recharge. Even Jesus had to get away from the thronging crowds daily to recharge.

Take time out for yourself. Get someone to take over for you at lease twice a week, so that you can have that alone time you need to recharge. Go to a movie, go see a play, see something funny. Laughter is a 'medicine' to your heart.

Take off with God two days a week, just you and him, and receive the peace and refreshing that he has in store for you.

Take yourself out to lunch and spend time with just you. You'll find that you might actually enjoy your own company. Just think, you will never keep you waiting around, or sitting by the phone, and there will never be any disagreements as to who pays the lunch bill. You will also find that you will never try to dominate the conversation or outdo yourself with the latest fashions. You're going to enjoy spending time with you!

Love's Just Aburnin'

Or, call up your friends and go to lunch with them! The most satisfying and rewarding thing you will ever receive as a caregiver, is taking time out for yourself, without apology.

It is during these times of refreshing, that you will come to realize who you really are in the Lord. Every caregiver needs time away to recharge.

> Psalms 23:1-3
> The Lord is my shepherd, and I shall not want. He makes me to lie down in green pastures, and He leads me beside the still waters. He restores my soul
>
> Psalm 27: 1
> The Lord is my light and my salvation: whom shall I fear? The Lord is the strength of my life; of whom shall I be afraid?

Don't be afraid of anyone or anything. Stay strong and don't think 'burnout.' Remember to always think 'burn-in.'

Love Takes Courage

Chapter 10

Love Takes Courage

Courage is the quality of being brave; the ability to face difficulty, uncertainty, or pain without being overcome by fear or being defected from a chosen course of action.

The truth of the matter is that God really cares for caregivers. Throughout all of my encounters as a caregiver, I can honestly say at the end of each situation I knew that it was only by the grace of God, with his mercy, courage compassion, love, willingness and obedience which took me all the way through.

No devil stopped anything, took anyone from me, or caused anything adverse to happen. Everything happened by God's divine plan. He is there for us, we just have to believe and step out. When we believe, then and only then will we be able to receive the rewards of our Father.

He is the lamp unto our feet and the one to talk to when things are not going so smoothly. Then it's time to stop, be quite and give thanks for everything that is going right.

It does not matter if you are the recipient's security-blanket protecting them from unwanted elements, or their teacher and mentor, or just a friend who loves them. No matter your involvement in care-giving, God is well pleased with your efforts! You have only to read Matthew Chapter 25 to know how true this is. And it is he alone that gives you the strength to carry on in your daily tasks.

Your courage alone is the gift that God has blessed you with to sustain your daily activities.

When we think of courage, we envision men and women going off to war to protect us, or firefighters who rescue us from an inferno. That same courage resides in each and everyone of us. It was placed their by God when He imparted his holy spirit in us, and is part of his divine nature.

> Deuteronomy 31:6
> Be strong and of good courage, fear not nor be afraid of them; for the Lord thy God, He is the one who will go with you. He will not fail you, nor leave you."

C - is for the care you put into your project

O - is for the outgoing attitude to continue

U - is for undertaking difficult projects

R - is for the realization of wanting to help

A - is for always being ready and reliable

G - is for the generosity you share

E - is for everything you do to console others

Love is Patient

Chapter 11

Love is Patient

Patience is the staying power, tolerance, persistence and the lack of complaint. In this chapter, I had to really examine myself. My very being was in question. Sometimes I got down right angry when I had to practice patience. You see, we never want to admit to other people that we don't have patience.

I can remember many times when my patience was severely tried. When I was on the streets helping the homeless, hurting and hungry people, I really learned what patience was. It was something I had to learn quite quickly.

If you didn't have patience with those people, they could sense it, and one could get hurt out on the streets without this quality.

Most of the time God sent people in my direction just to see what level my patience was set at. I truly believe that there are many levels. The first level is holding patience. This is where you would like to just knock someone out for acting up. Then you hear from God and He reminds you why you are there. He reminds you to hold your peace and that you are there to help others.

> Luke 19:10
> For the son of man has come to seek and save those who are lost.

So then I would have to take time out to pray and go back to that person with a different attitude. Before long, God places you into the next level. Level two is showing patience as kindness, longsuffering and loving deeds. This is the level when your patience is on a good display to those around you. You know you have reached level two when you don't have to take a 'time out' from the person you are helping.

Love is Patient

You also know you are there when you are better able to handle the situation without getting upset and angry. I am sure there are many additional levels of patience and as we stay in prayer and humility, God will reveal our levels to us.

God is letting us know that we must practice patience and the ability to endure hardships. Patience is something we are born with; however, some of us just don't expose it as well as others.

> Ecclesiastes 7:8-9
> Better is the end of a thing than the beginning thereof: And the patient in spirit is better than the proud in spirit. Be not hasty in your spirit to be angry; for anger rests in the bosom of fools.

> 1st Timothy 6:11
> But you, oh man of God, flee these things; and follow after righteousness, godliness, faith, love patience, meekness.

James 5: 7-8

Be patient therefore, brethren, until the coming of the Lord. Behold the farmer waits for the precious fruit of the earth, and has long patience for it until he receives the early and latter rain. Let your patience be the same also; establish your hearts for the coming of the Lord draws near.

Revelation 3:10

Because you have kept the word of My patience, I also will keep you from the hour of temptation, which shall come upon the entire world to try them that dwell upon the earth.

All these things are part of our life's patience. It's a practice we must all endure. I saw the levels of my patience grow when I began to care for senior citizens. They are a species all their own.

One of my cases was a woman with Alzheimer's disease and cancer. When I started care-giving for her, the cancer wasn't yet the controlling factor in her body.

Love is Patient

It was the irrational, unpredictable behavior and stubbornness of Alzheimer's that thoroughly tested me, and my patience took a stand.

One day as I was caring for her, she pushed me down, catching me totally off guard. I fell very hard to the floor. While I was down, she kicked me in my breast. I was in so much pain, I thought I would pass out. There was nothing I could do but endure the pain and shock, and to be patient, hoping that her rage subsided quickly.

When I caught my breath, I realized that I was on the floor, and I had to become very longsuffering. That's when I knew my patience had really kicked in. The only thing I could do was to call on God, regroup and get myself together. I had to come to terms with the fact that she was sick.

Another time as I was dressing her, she hit me so hard it again almost knocked me to the ground. I had to struggle to keep my balance and stop myself from toppling over into the floor yet again. People with Alzheimer's disease have a lot of strength during a certain stage of their illness. Again, I had to come to terms with the fact that she did not know what she was doing.

As her disease progressed, other actions were caused by her illness. I remember one time I had cooked a delicious meal for her, and as I prepared her plate she refused to eat and emptied the entire plate all over the floor. And then she stepped in the spilled food, mashing it into the floor!

During these events, although abusive and sometimes quite violent, I still maintained a level of patience which only a true care giver can display. Such activities will truly test your patience, and God will always remind you of your patience, and be there to witness how you are using that portion of patience He blessed you with.

On the following page is a God-inspired poem for your reading pleasure.

Love is Patient

PATIENCE

When you are at your very end
Surely there will be a Friend
Who makes a lasting mark
To stay at your side
With the racing of time
The calm in your heart
It was there from the start
That's when you hold it in
Congratulations!
Patience, you have won again.

Love's Endurance

Chapter 12

Love's Endurance

Strength coupled with courage brings on resilience, and resilience is the element that will confirm for you that you have guts, fortitude and stamina to carry on and endure pain.

One's endurance is always put to the test when they have to take care of another. When I began to take care of my Aunt Helen, I really found out what endurance was all about. This was my first introduction to the enduring side of care-giving.

One of the hardest things to endure is loneliness. These are the times when you feel that no one in the world ever cares for you. It's because you are so isolated with the recipient. Most of the time you forget about yourself because you are consumed with the task of being there for someone else. Enduring the lonely times when there is no one around but you and the recipient, is something you will have to get passed in order to be effective.

I remember times when I did not see anyone or even go outside for days at a time. I think that's when I found out 'who really cares for the caregivers. God in His greatness showed up and embraced me during those times of loneliness. That was when I learned who really cared for me.

When I prayed in his presence I was filled with an unspeakable outpouring of his joy in my Life. I didn't need any other replacement. When I felt lonely I found myself immersed in his presence. God's reward is expressed brilliantly here in such times. You may sometimes become tempted to cop an attitude with the one you are caring for, but you must remember that "blessed is the man who endures temptation."

Love's Endurance

>James 1:12
>Blessed is the man that endures temptation; for when he is tried, he shall receive the crown of life, which the lord has promised to them that love him.

>2nd Timothy 4:7-8
>I have fought a good fight, I have finished my course, and I have kept the faith; Hereafter there is laid up for me a crown of righteousness, which the Lord, the righteous judge shall give me at that day and not to me only but to all them also that love His appearing.

This now brings me to a young woman by the name of Dezi, who happens to be one of my favorite people. She has for so many years shown me what endurance is all about. She is also a caregiver with perfect love. I've watched her care not only for children, but for so many others in different situations. Some of the things I have watched her endure were differently orchestrated by God, in order to design her destiny.

In her care-giving, she got injured and experienced much pain, but she kept the faith and remained with

God through it all. She endured with love and is without a doubt my role model of endurance. I have learned the true purpose of endurance by watching this young woman deal with many of her own life's situations, and witnessed each time God's love, mercy, peace and endurance bring her through it all. I now know for a fact that endurance is not something we are born with, but something we must develop over our life time. To endure is to set aside one's self. Always remember that endurance is the art of you holding on.

Endurance

E - is for the energy you put into what you do

D - is for the dedication to your task

U - is for the unselfishness you show to all

R - is your readiness and willingness

A - is your great attitude at all times

N - is never quitting

C - is the calm and peace you bring in a storm

E - is your everlasting love for what you do

*Who Cares
for the Caregiver?*

Chapter 13

Who Cares for the Caregiver?

I often reflected back on my friend, Naomi, and can still see her smiling face in my memory. I knew she was smiling down on me, as I went forth to help others.

Being a caregiver requires a certain type of attitude. You must show an attitude of love. Hurting people always sense 'genuine assistance.' I have given more than thirty years of my life here in Los Angeles, California, or if you prefer, even more taking into consideration my years as a teen when I used to help my grandmother care for others. In those days, she was the caregiver and I was just her helper.

She began by caring for my grandfather who had a stroke. She brought him home from the hospital, and would not allow him to go into an institution. She kept him in his own environment and we took care of him at home until he died.

I learned a great deal from my quite, soft-spoken grandmother. Everyone loved her because she shared the meanings of love, kindness, compassion, joy, honesty and integrity with them. I watched as she cared for others and wondered why she always gave of herself so much.

Some forty years later, I understood the how-tos and whys of her work. It was a God-driven thing. The more I reflected on my grandmother it became abundantly clear to me why we do what we do. So I asked myself the question:

"As caregivers, where can we go when *we* need help? Who can we talk to when we need to unload?"

I found that invariably my help came from the Lord, so I immersed myself daily in the word. I stood on his word every spare moment I had, and one day, God took me to these passages of scripture:

> Psalm 33:20
> Our soul waits for the Lord; He is our help and our shield.

> Psalm 22: 19
> But be not far from me, oh Lord, oh my strength; make haste to help me.

I would also like to share this word with caregivers:

> Psalm 124: 8
> Our help is in the name of the Lord, who makes heaven and earth.

I found that seeking the soothing comfort of his word was the only help forthcoming to me. You see, there are not many people who are willing to help you when you can't give them something in return. People are just like that. It's their nature. Being a true caregiver is when the people you help cannot give you anything in return.

In an effort to stay focused and strong for the work that God gave me, I began to watch Christian television, Christian DVDs and listen to God's music, as much as I could, because in the presence of the Lord is strength for one's being, especially in this line of work. And yet, the question still haunted me.

"Who cares for the caregiver?"

The answer is always, "God does." Sometimes it's easy to lose sight of this, and we may not want to believe that we still need more. At such times, the caregiver must remember that He cares for us even when we don't care of ourselves. He cares for us even when we think He has forgotten us. He cares when we are in trouble and don't know which way is out. He cares for us when we are lonely with no one to talk to.

I began to think about all the people in our universe who have no one to take care of them. Many have illnesses that most of us would rather not be around, ranging from mental disorders, old age, dementia, Alzheimer's, cancer, and AIDS, just to name a few.

Who Cares for the Caregiver?

Some of these people are living on the streets of our cities and in our neighborhoods. When we see them, we mutter to ourselves, "Oh, look at how he/she is acting," when we should be taking the time to see how we can help.

Did we ever stop to think that some of these people are suffering from one of the above mentioned diseases? Did we ever consider a method of helping, or perhaps becoming a caregiver?

I once came across a person that needed help and thought that he/she was suffering from mental illness, when in fact he/she had Alzheimer's disease; a medical disorder causing a degenerative dementia affecting the brain, especially late in life.

Some of these affected persons are in the latent, violent stages of their diseases, which only resemble the effects of mental illness. I remember helping a person with Alzheimer's disease who became very violent. I was hit very hard and knocked to the ground. It was only the love of God that got me through the situation.

Had I not researched the behaviors of this disease and determined the true problem, this person would have been labeled as mentally ill and locked away in an institution. That was another point in my life where I accepted that I was a caregiver.

As caring for others since 1974, I found it to be very rewarding and found that I have a great desire within my heart and soul to help others. To share my love is sharing God's love. God has truly blessed me for helping others.

I never once helped anyone for the express purpose of being blessed in return, and yet the Lord blesses me all the time, anyway. It's just the way He intended it to be. He is the one that cares for the caregiver with everlasting rewards.

We hope that you enjoyed Dr. Landry's profound reflections on care-giving. May this book bring refreshment to other caregivers and visitors, alike.

If you would like to correspond with Dr. Landry, order additional copies of this issue, or book speaking engagements, please visit:

glandrybook@gmail.com

To order additional copies online, go to:
Amazon.com/books
In the search box, enter: Dr. G Landry

To receive announcements concerning future books and events, please visit Dr. Landry at:

www.caregiversspeaks.org

To receive a free copy of
Black Americans and Cancer
Please mail a check or money order for $2.50
for shipping & handling to:

P.O. Box 73843 Los Angeles CA. 90003
Or call: 323-788-3124

A Prayer for the Care-giver

Psalm 20

May the Lord hear you in the day of trouble

May the God of Jacob defend you

And send you help from His sanctuary

May He strengthen you out of Zion

May He remember all your offerings

And accept your burned sacrifices

May He grant you according to your

Heart's desire and fulfill all your petitions!

Amen.

Credits

Page 65: Biblical Discernment Ministries, December, 1997

www.ingramcontent.com/pod-product-compliance
Lightning Source LLC
Chambersburg PA
CBHW071134090426
42736CB00012B/2125